TUDOR
1485-1603

STUART
1603-1714

GEORGIAN
1714-1837

children's HISTORY of NOTTINGHAMSHIRE

Written by
Ian Douglas

HOMETOWN WORLD

How well do you know your town?

Have you ever wondered what it would have been like living in Nottingham's caves? What about meeting Robin Hood in Sherwood Forest? This book will uncover the important and exciting things that have happened in Nottinghamshire.

Want to hear the other good bits? You will love this book! Some rather brainy folk have worked on it to make sure it's fun and informative. So what are you waiting for? Peel back the pages and be amazed at the story of your county.

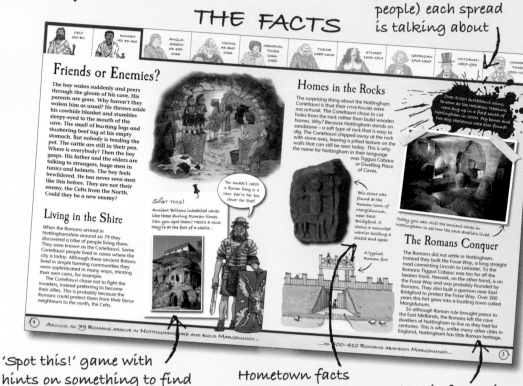

THE FACTS

Timeline shows which period (dates and people) each spread is talking about

'Spot this!' game with hints on something to find

Hometown facts to amaze you!

Clear informative text

THE EVIDENCE

Intriguing old photos

Each period in the book ends with a summary explaining how we know about the past.

Go back in time to find out what it was like for children growing up in Nottinghamshire.

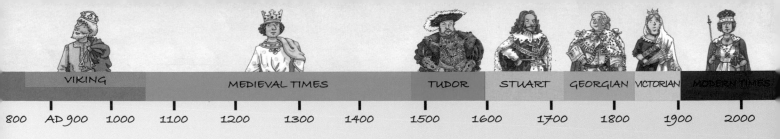

Contents

CELT
500 BC

ROMAN
AD 43-410

ANGLO-
SAXON
AD 450-
1066

VIKING
AD 865-
1066

MEDIEV
TIME
1066
148

Friends or Enemies?

The boy wakes suddenly and peers through the gloom of his cave. His parents are gone. Why haven't they woken him as usual? He throws aside his cowhide blanket and stumbles sleepy-eyed to the mouth of the cave. The smell of burning logs and simmering beef tug at his empty stomach. But nobody is tending the pot. The cattle are still in their pen. Where is everybody? Then the boy gasps. His father and the elders are talking to strangers, huge men in tunics and helmets. The boy feels bewildered. He has never seen men like this before. They are not their enemy, the Celts from the North. Could they be a new enemy?

Living in the Shire

When the Romans arrived in Nottinghamshire around AD 79 they discovered a tribe of people living there. They were known as the Corieltauvi. Some Corieltauvi people lived in caves where the city is today. Although these ancient Britons lived in simple farming communities they were sophisticated in many ways, minting their own coins, for example.

The Corieltauvi chose not to fight the invaders, instead preferring to become their allies. This is probably because the Romans could protect them from their fierce neighbours to the north, the Celts.

You wouldn't catch a Roman living in a cave. We're far too clever for that!

SPOT THIS!

Ancient Britons inhabited caves like these during Roman times. Can you spot them? Here's a clue: they're at the foot of a castle...

TUDOR
1485-1603

STUART
1603-1714

GEORGIAN
1714-1837

VICTORIAN
1837-1901

MODERN
TIMES
1902-NOW

Homes in the Rocks

The surprising thing about the Nottingham Corieltauvi is that their cave homes were not natural. The Corieltauvi chose to cut holes from the rock rather than build wooden homes. Why? Because Nottingham stands on sandstone – a soft type of rock that is easy to dig. The Corieltauvi chipped away at the rock with stone axes, leaving a pitted texture on the walls that can still be seen today. This is why the name for Nottingham in their language was Tiggua Cabauc or Dwelling Place of Caves.

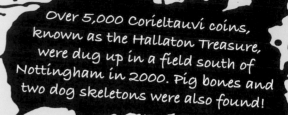
Over 5,000 Corieltauvi coins, known as the Hallaton Treasure, were dug up in a field south of Nottingham in 2000. Pig bones and two dog skeletons were also found!

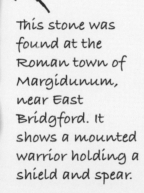
This stone was found at the Roman town of Margidunum, near East Bridgford. It shows a mounted warrior holding a shield and spear.

Today you can visit the ancient caves in Nottingham to see how the cave-dwellers lived.

The Romans Conquer

The Romans did not settle in Nottingham. Instead they built the Fosse Way, a long straight road connecting Lincoln to Leicester. To the Romans Tiggua Cabauc was too far off the beaten track. Newark, on the other hand, is on the Fosse Way and was probably founded by Romans. They also built a garrison near East Bridgford to protect the Fosse Way. Over 300 years this fort grew into a bustling town called Margidunum.

So although Roman rule brought peace to the East Midlands, the Romans left the cave dwellers of Nottingham to live as they had for centuries. This is why, unlike many other cities in England, Nottingham has little Roman heritage.

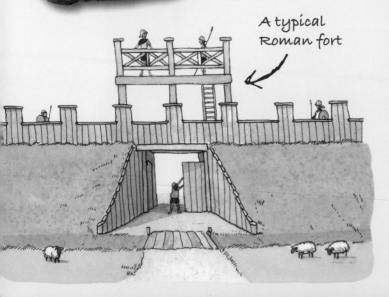
A typical Roman fort

CELT
500 BC

ROMAN
AD 43-410

ANGLO-
SAXON
AD 450-
1066

VIKING
AD 865-
1066

MEDIEV
TIME
1066
1485

What did the clean, civilised Romans make of Nottingham's cave dwellers? Both sides must have had quite a culture shock. Here is an imaginary account by 10 year-old Alec – a Corieltauvi boy on a trip to Margidunum.

Keep near me, son, or the Romans might kidnap you!

It took our canoe half the day to reach Margidunum from Tiggua Cabauc. After all that paddling my muscles burned like fire. And we saw three wolves along the way!

Margidunum is a peculiar place – all those tree trunks chopped down and wedged together to make battlements. I felt afraid and Father told me to stay close. If the Romans thought I was an orphan they might take me for their slave!

Four enormous soldiers guarded the entrance. Father showed them our beef carcasses and they gestured for us to pass. Inside were more of their funny buildings. Plastered walls with clay tiles for a roof. I looked through a window and saw a shiny floor made from tiny tiles. Caves aren't good enough for the Romans!

The Romans wanted to buy our food but Father couldn't agree a deal. They will only pay with their foreign coins and not Corieltauvi. The Romans say our money is worthless and we must change if we want to survive.

Things like pottery, bones and coins provide evidence so archaeologists can work out where the Romans lived.

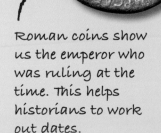

Roman coins show us the emperor who was ruling at the time. This helps historians to work out dates.

TUDOR
1485-1603

STUART
1603-1714

GEORGIAN
1714-1837

VICTORIAN
1837-1901

MODERN
TIMES
1902-NOW

Experts have looked at the remains of Roman villas at Margidunum and have been able to draw plans, showing the location and purpose of each room.

Plans can be used to make models of Roman villas, like this one.

How do we know?

Corieltauvi coins, pottery and other historic objects are often uncovered in Nottinghamshire when the foundations of new houses are being dug. In the city these objects are often mixed with Roman items. So although the Romans didn't settle in Nottingham, the two cultures must have made contact quite often.

Lots of Roman artefacts have been found at Margidunum, the Roman town near East Bridgford. Digging in the 1960s, archaeologists found at least 22 buildings in Margidunum, dating from Roman times. As well as homes, there were workshops, trading stalls and a bathhouse with underfloor heating.

A Roman villa excavated in Mansfield revealed painted walls and mosaic floors. It probably belonged to a Roman farming family who enjoyed eating well. The remains of oysters and deer, along with wine glasses, were dug up from the foundations.

Archaeologists have been digging for over 100 years at Margidunum.

A Hard Life

The mother weeps as she looks at her son's empty bed. This is their first night without him. He was outside chopping the firewood this morning when they broke the news. When she remembers the look on his face, she cries aloud. But the handful of coins the slave trader paid for their son will keep the other children alive until spring. Her husband tried to comfort her by saying that their son is going to Snotengaham, where a new master will feed and clothe him. In a way, he said, their son is lucky.

Nottingham's Beginning

Oh yes, we all love Snot around here. Snot is very powerful!

The Saxons settled on a hill where the Lace Market is situated today. The steep sides made it easy to defend and the River Trent was useful for transport. This colony became known as Snotengaham, meaning 'the home of Snot's people'. Snot was probably one of the first village chieftains.

Most Saxons were farmers and many also settled in the fertile Trent Valley. There were no schools and children worked long days on the farm. In the evenings they played with knucklebone dice, dolls made from wood and rags, or told stories about brave warriors and monsters.

SPOT THIS!

This cross stands in a Stapleford churchyard. It's about 1,300 years old! 'Stapul' is the Anglo-Saxon word for 'post'. Can you see how Stapleford got its name?

...AROUND AD 600 SAXONS SETTLE HERE...AD 700-800 MERCIA BECOMES IMPORTAN

TUDOR
1485-1603

STUART
1603-1714

GEORGIAN
1714-1837

VICTORIAN
1837-1901

MODERN
TIMES
1902-NOW

The Rise of Mercia

Snotengaham was in the kingdom of Mercia, in the Midlands. King Penda tried to make Mercia powerful by fighting rival kingdoms. Fighting continued for over a century until King Offa defeated the enemy to become Mercia's most successful monarch. This made Offa very wealthy and allowed him to forge Britain's first gold coins. The Wessex king Egbert conquered Mercia after Offa's death and is said to have built Newark castle.

Ordinary Mercians, however, were very poor and were known to sell their children into slavery. This sounds cruel, but during famines it made sure the child survived. Slavery was not necessarily for life. Family members could buy a slave's freedom.

Snotengaham was just a small farming village in Saxon times.

Map of Angle-Land AD 600-900

PICTLAND

STRATHCLYDE

Hadrian's Wall

NORTHUMBRIA

LINDSEY

MERCIA

EAST ANGLIA

HWICCA

ESSEX

WESSEX

KENT

SUSSEX

N

This map shows Mercia and the other kingdoms in Anglo-Saxon England.

How do we know?

In 1936, builders unearthed a Saxon wall near Bridlesmith Gate in Nottingham. When archaeologists explored further they found a dungeon with steps, chambers and a deep smooth pit impossible to escape.

We know the Saxons had a Christian church at Southwell because its bricks were used to build the famous Southwell Minster. Place names are another clue. For example, the 'ton' in Sutton-in-Ashfield, Gamston and Laxton comes from their Saxon origins, meaning 'an enclosure'.

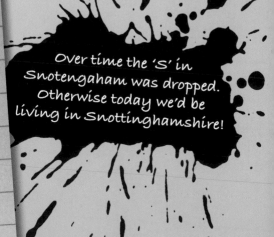

Over time the 'S' in Snotengaham was dropped. Otherwise today we'd be living in Snottinghamshire!

CELT
500 BC

ROMAN
AD 43-410

ANGLO-
SAXON
AD 450-
1066

VIKING
AD 865-
1066

MEDIE
TIME
1066
148

Here Come the Vikings!

The early morning mist has lifted from the River Trent. A young Saxon girl is out picking wild herbs when suddenly, the sound of shouts and swishing oars catches her attention. From behind a rock, the girl watches as an enormous Viking longboat sails into view. The men onboard call out in a strange language. It must be Norse! The girl's heart sinks as she realises the rumour is true. The King has given her village, Snotengaham, to the Vikings!

Mercia Defeated

The Mercian King Burghred was surrounded by enemies. The king of Wessex was threatening to invade and, to make matters worse, there was talk of an uprising by Burghred's own subjects. Then the Viking armies arrived from the north. In return for peace, Burghred gave them Snotengaham. Perhaps he hoped an alliance with the Vikings would discourage Wessex from attacking. If this was his plan it backfired. Within ten years the Vikings were in control of Mercia.

Real Viking shoes!

SOT THIS!

Have you been here shopping? A cave beneath this street used to be a forge. Gata is the Norse word for 'street' so Bridlesmith Gate – or 'street of the bridlesmiths' – has Viking roots.

The Danelaw

The large area of eastern England conquered by the Vikings became known as the 'Danelaw' because people had to live by Danish rules and justice. The Danes divided this area into modern counties, including Nottinghamshire.

Many Nottinghamshire villages still have Danish names today, such as those ending in 'thorpe' – which means 'farm' in Danish – like Bilsthorpe, Newthorpe and Sibthorpe.

Becoming a Town

The Anglo-Saxon Chronicle is a record of key events in Saxon and Viking times.

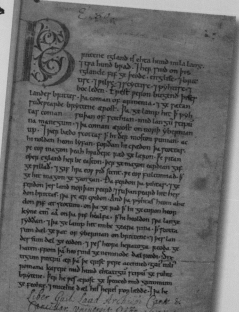

The Vikings probably wanted Nottingham because its hillsides made it easy to protect. Over the next few decades they fortified the town with garrisons and huge battlements. But these preparations failed when King Edward's English army recaptured the city. To make sure the Vikings did not return, Edward strengthened the city's defences. These reinforcements turned Nottingham from a village to an important town.

Viking helmets did not have horns, as people often believe.

Many Vikings settled here, raised families and became communities.

How do we know?

Monks were among the few people at this time who could read or write. The Anglo-Saxon Chronicle is a collection of manuscripts, handwritten by monks from the 9th to the 12th century. They describe important events including the Viking occupation of Mercia.

Another source comes from a Welsh monk called Asser. He visited Viking Nottingham and wrote about the town and its history.

The ground below the Lace Market contains the foundations of Viking wooden houses. These show us that the Vikings increased the size of Snotengaham. The largest house was over 12 metres long. This could have been a meeting hall where Vikings drank ale and told stories. Among the items discovered in the Lace Market were a decorated belt buckle and a bronze top from a staff — a popular Viking weapon.

CELT
500 BC

ROMAN
AD 43-410

ANGLO-SAXON
AD 450-1066

VIKING
AD 865-1066

MEDIEV
TIME
1066-1

Kidnapped!

Hooves clip on cobblestones as horses approach the Castle Gate. Among the riders a boy lifts his head and stares at grey battlements. His heart shivers. He has been kidnapped by King John's soldiers. His father is a supporter of John's enemies. Unless his father swears allegiance to the King the boy will be killed. He cries as he thinks of his family. Will he ever escape Nottingham Castle?

A New Castle

William the Conqueror ordered the building of a wooden castle in Nottingham to strengthen his defences. The Normans settled outside the castle at Hounds Gate, which was known as the French Borough. The people spoke French and lived by French laws.

The Lace Market where the Saxons lived became known as the English Borough. The Saxons must have found it strange working alongside their new French neighbours.

A century passed and a stronger stone castle replaced the wooden one. The caves underneath made suitable dungeons. Meanwhile, outside the city, the Normans fortified Newark Castle and built Southwell Minster.

SPOT THIS!

Do you recognise these 'pepperpot' spires? This well-known minster in Nottinghamshire was built in medieval times.

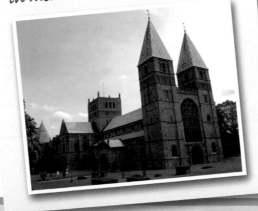

Murder and Treason

Richard the Lionheart returned from the crusades to find his brother John plotting against him. John moved into Nottingham Castle for protection but King Richard led his soldiers in a daring attack and overcame the castle's fortifications. He made John his prisoner but later released him.

After Richard's death, John became king. He was unpopular and his barons rebelled. So he imprisoned 28 of their sons, aged 12 to 14, at Nottingham. The plan was to force the barons into obedience. Instead the barons became even more determined to defeat the king. So he ordered the boys to be hanged. For this and other evil acts King John was very unpopular and in 1215 he was forced to promise certain legal rights to his people. These were laid down in the Magna Carta and are still part of English law today.

TUDOR
1485-1603

STUART
1603-1714

GEORGIAN
1714-1837

VICTORIAN
1837-1901

MODERN
TIMES
1902-
NOW

A Secret Cave

John was not the only king to make use of Nottingham Castle. In 1327 Queen Isabella and a nobleman called Roger Mortimer lived there, after killing King Edward II. Edward's son became Edward III, but Queen Isabella and Mortimer were England's real rulers. Then one night while everyone was sleeping, 17 year-old Edward and his followers crept into the castle through a secret cave. They captured Isabella and had Mortimer executed.

Nottingham became even more important when it had a castle.

This model inside Nottingham Castle shows what the castle looked like in the 16th century.

The Domesday Book recorded who held all the land and wealth in England in 1086. This copy of the document shows Nottingham's old name at the top.

How do we know?

In medieval times, monks kept records of important events by writing them down. A few monks even became great historians.

Monks living at Rufford Abbey 950 years ago wrote with feather quills to make copies of letters and charters. In 1471 John, Abbot of Rufford, compiled over 300 years' worth of documents. One of the most outrageous events was a kidnapping in 1317 by some Abbey monks for a ransom of £200!

Medieval records tell us a lot about everyday life in Nottinghamshire. For example, in the 14th century it was a crime to drop litter and to gossip! Many of these records are stored today in the Nottinghamshire Archives Office.

CELT
500 BC

ROMAN
AD 43-410

ANGLO-
SAXON
AD 450-
1066

VIKING
AD 865-
1066

MEDIEV
TIME
1066-1

Robyn Hode

The minstrel is tuning his harp at a Tudor banquet. The guests are well fed, drunk and bored. If he disappoints them they may refuse his fee. Luckily he knows a ballad that is guaranteed to please. It tells the story of a great archer outlawed to Sherwood Forest who, with the giant Little John, formed a group of warriors called the Merry Men. Together they fought the evil Sheriff of Nottingham, stealing his wealth to give to the poor.

"Lythe and listin, gentilmen,
That be of frebore blode;
I shall you tel of a gode yeoman,
His name was Robyn Hode."

> Hey, I know that song! It's from 'A Gest of Robyn Hode'!

Man or Myth?

There is no proof that Robin Hood ever lived in Sherwood Forest. It's folklore – a traditional story passed down over centuries.

After a long day of backbreaking toil, medieval people wanted entertainment. Most people couldn't read so listening to stories and songs was a good way to have fun. But why did the Ballads of Robin Hood become so popular? Probably because it's a perfect story. A hero, wronged by a wicked villain, loses everything. He fights back by being brave and fair. In the end he wins and gets the girl!

New generations added to the story, keeping it alive and exciting. Friar Tuck was not in the early versions, but his jolly character brought a touch of comedy. King John, known for his villainy in real life, was woven into the plot, making it more believable.

SPOT THIS!
This Robin Hood statue makes a popular snapshot for visitors to Nottingham. Where is it?

TUDOR
1485-1603

STUART
1603-1714

GEORGIAN
1714-1837

VICTORIAN
1837-1901

MODERN
TIMES
1902-
NOW

Local Legend

Over time the story grew and was adapted for books, film and television, capturing the imagination of people across the world. As Robin's name grew, Nottinghamshire also became more famous. The story turned the county into a major tourist destination. Local people named locations after his legend. Today you can drive down Maid Marian Way or eat at the Robin Hood Restaurant.

The Major Oak in Sherwood Forest is thought to have been Robin Hood's headquarters!

Robin Hood is often shown fighting with a sword. But in medieval times only rich men had swords so it's unlikely that Robin Hood had one.

Robin Hood and Little John fight each other using sticks called staffs in this engraving from 1869.

How do we know?

The name Robert Hod appears a lot in court records from the 13th century. But as these records span many towns and years, the references can't all be about the same man. Robert Hod simply means Robert with a hood. The hood was a common headdress back then. But it is possible that these references inspired the early tales.

By the 14th century, minstrels were singing ballads of Robin's adventures. Copies of ballads from the 15th and 16th centuries have survived, showing us how the story changed. The first printed edition was 'A Gest of Robyn Hode' in 1475. Playwright Anthony Mundy put on two Robin plays at the end of the 16th century. These show Robin as a nobleman, rather than the poor man of the ballads.

Although the stories can be traced through the ages, we can't prove Robin Hood was real. But we can't prove he was fake either!

...1475 'A GEST OF ROBYN HODE' IS PRINTED FOR THE FIRST TIME...

(15)

Danger at the Priory

The young novice hides out of sight as soldiers break down the door of Lenton Priory. They are looking for Father Nicholas, the head friar. The King's men claim he is a traitor plotting against the Crown. But the Father insists he is an innocent man, wrongly accused by heretics. The novice fears Nicholas will be found guilty and executed. Then the King can close the Priory and seize its assets. The novice will be homeless. Trembling, he prays for Father Nicholas's safety.

A War Ends

A Battle at East Stoke marked the end in Nottinghamshire of the Wars of the Roses. Henry VII, the first Tudor king, was now secure on the throne. In 1529 his son, Henry VIII, wanted a divorce, which was against the Church's beliefs. So Henry broke the connection with the Pope in Rome and created a new Church of England. The king ordered all monasteries and other religious houses to be closed and seized the land belonging to them. This was called the Dissolution of the Monasteries. Lenton Priory and Beauvale Priory were two local monasteries closed by the Dissolution.

Do you know which famous Henry this is? ←

Lenton Priory

Lenton Priory was 400 years old by the time of the Tudors. In 1538 the prior, Nicholas Heath, and 12 others were arrested on charges of treason. Whether he was really guilty was never made clear. Prior Nicholas was hanged and the priory was closed. The buildings were demolished and some of the stone was used to build Wollaton Hall nearby. Today, Lenton Abbey takes its name from the vanished priory

← *Lenton Priory was destroyed by Henry VIII*

...1487 BATTLE OF STOKE...1538 HENRY VIII'S MEN DESTROY LENTON PRIORY.

Plague!

Another great danger for Tudor Nottingham was the plague. There were outbreaks every few years from 1558 to 1647, known locally as 'the Visitations'. Strangers were turned away from the town's gates, even healthy people seeking to escape the disease. Residents were forbidden to leave. Stray dog and cats were slaughtered, pigs had to be kept inside the home and pubs were shut. Sadly the precautions always failed and many people died.

During the plague, dead and dying people were thrown into the castle caves and left to rot. Eww!

Royalists were also known as Cavaliers. The Parliamentarians were called Roundheads.

Spot this!

Roundheads and Cavaliers recruited soldiers in this Nottingham pub. But luckily they weren't there at the same time! Do you know where it is?

A Growing Town

Despite these troubles Nottingham prospered and the population grew. Many of the streets in the modern city centre such as Weekday Cross, Angel Row and Long Row were the homes of craftsmen and traders. They made goods in small workshops behind their houses and sold them from shops on the ground floor.

In villages like Strelley and Wollaton, coal mining was expanding. Pits were sunk to the shallow seams of coal that were close to the surface.

A cross like this marked the site of one of Nottingham's markets in the medieval and Tudor times.

Another War Begins

Nottinghamshire played an important role when the Civil War broke out in 1642. The Civil War was a struggle between Royalists, who were loyal to the king, and Parliamentarians, who wanted to limit the king's powers.

The War started in 1642 when King Charles I was in Nottingham. He rode to the Castle and had his flag flown from its highest tower, signalling men to join his army.

Nottinghamshire was divided between the two sides. The Parliamentarians took control of Nottingham, while Newark was controlled by Royalists. The King was eventually captured at Southwell when the Minster was damaged in the fighting.

After the Parliamentarians won the war they had Nottingham's castle destroyed, to make sure the Royalists never used it again. They also devastated Newark Castle.

CELT
500 BC

ROMAN
AD 43-410

ANGLO-
SAXON
AD 450-
1066

VIKING
AD 865-
1066

MEDIE
TIM
106
148

Nottingham has celebrated the Goose Fair for over 700 years. In Tudor times the fair took place on St Matthew's Day, September 21st. But how did St Matthew's Fair compare to today's festival? Read 10 year-old Jane's imaginary visit to the fair. What is different? Is anything the same?

Some of the geese had waddled their way from Norfolk!

Father kindly allowed us the day off for St Matthew's Fair, once the chores were done. I've never scrubbed laundry so fast in my life!

The crowds were huge as we walked down Long Row. Ma gave me permission to run ahead. "Behave yourself and don't talk to strangers," she said. Then she handed me a whole farthing to spend!

There was so much to see! Market Square was full of colourful stalls, with smoke billowing into the air. A nobleman's feast hung in that smoke, with the smell of pork, beef and fowl cooking on bonfires. There were cheeses of all shapes and sizes. And there were animals for sale too: horses, sheep, cows and hundreds of geese. Drunken people kept tripping over the geese and swearing. That made me laugh.

I bought a goose wing and listened to the flutes and harps of the minstrels. One fiddle-player sang the Ballad of Robin Hood. Among the other entertainments were fortune-tellers, dancing bears, and people with strange physiques.

St Matthew's is the most exciting day. I can't wait for next year!

These crowds are watching people on a new ride called the Cake Walk in 1908.

Taken in 2008, this photo shows the Goose Fair 100 years later.

TUDOR
1485-
1603

STUART
1603-1714

GEORGIAN
1714-
1837

VICTORIAN
1837-1901

MODERN
TIMES
1902-NOW

This is the flag of King Charles, flown at Nottingham Castle at the start of the Civil War.

How do we know?

In the past, writing a letter was often the best way to get a message to someone. The Tudor men closing the monasteries wrote to the king to keep him updated. However, as it was their job to force out the monks, their stories about monks behaving badly can't all be believed! Other documents such as wills, tax returns and parish registers also tell us about life in Tudor Nottinghamshire.

We know King Charles raised his flag at the Castle at the start of the Civil War because there is an account from his court trial. Witnesses gave evidence describing that fateful night.

We can also learn a lot from local historians. Dr Thoroton was a doctor in Nottinghamshire in the 17th century. He loved history and wrote a book about the history of the county. He describes visits to places like Lenton Priory and gives eyewitness accounts of local events.

In the 17th century it was unusual for a woman to travel around the country but Celia Fiennes did just that. She toured England and kept a diary of her adventures. She visited Nottingham in 1697, describing it as 'the neatest town I have seen.' She describes the town and praises Nottingham ale!

Nottingham was a busy and growing town in Tudor and Stuart times.

Dr Thoroton wrote an important local history book. Today the county's main local history society is named after him.

Anger on the Streets

The castle is burning! The boy grips his father's hand tightly. From the safety of Market Square they watch as flames light the sky. Crowds fill the streets, some running away, others coming to look. Angry rioters started the fire, furious that the government denied them the right to vote. With a great roar the roof collapses. People cheer and wave their fists in the air. The boy feels confused. Can life in Nottinghamshire ever be the same after this?

Great Change

Nottinghamshire changed a lot during the 19th century. Steam power and other new technology meant things could be done more quickly and on a bigger scale. New machines made mass-production possible. This exciting time in history is known as the Industrial Revolution.

The Victorians' main fuel was coal. Everywhere from poor households to palaces needed it for heating. Engineers learned how to dig deep shafts to reach the coal underground. As a result coalmining quickly spread across Nottinghamshire. Mining villages like Eastwood, Newstead and Kimberley grew up around the collieries.

Busy Factories

From about 1820 Nottingham became the main centre in Britain for the manufacture of lace by machines. Previously lace had been made by hand. Many large factories were built and lace was sent all over the world from warehouses in the Lace Market. Nottingham's lace became famous. From about 1850 machines were used in another old Nottingham craft: hosiery knitting.

The Raleigh Company set up the largest bicycle making works in the world in Lenton. Meanwhile, a local herbalist – Jesse Boot – turned his chemist shop into a nationwide business: Boots.

This drawing from 1840 shows women working on lace embroidery in Nottingham

Riot!

The Duke of Newcastle didn't repair the castle after the fire in 1831.

People left the countryside to take factory jobs. Wages were low and working conditions were harsh, so workers campaigned for better treatment. They also wanted more people to be able to vote. But the government didn't want to change the way the country was run. There was widespread anger in many towns.

In 1831 angry rioters set fire to Colwick Hall and Nottingham Castle. They marched as far as Wollaton Hall where volunteer soldiers broke up the rioters. Eventually the government gave in and passed a Reform Act so that more people could vote.

Nottingham Castle, owned by the Duke of Newcastle, was in ruins after the fire. Nottingham residents were ordered to pay taxes to rebuild the castle but the Duke decided to abandon it.

SPOT THIS!

Feargus O'Connor fought to give workers the right to vote. He became MP for Nottingham in 1847. Can you find his statue in Arboretum Park?

The City Council repaired the castle and reopened it as a public art gallery in 1878.

New Houses

The increase in population led to rapid house building. Neighbourhoods around Nottingham such as St Ann's, Sneinton and Hyson Green developed dramatically. But housing was overcrowded, without baths, toilets or running water. Not surprisingly people's health suffered, and outbreaks of cholera were common in the first half of the century.

From the 1860s onwards Nottingham City Corporation began 'slum clearance,' replacing insanitary houses with better quality homes. Pumping stations like Papplewick piped clean water into the city. Drains were installed to empty toilets. Meanwhile the Arboretum was built as somewhere to get fresh air. By the 1880s Nottingham's health was improving.

Two huge beam engines at Papplewick pumped water from a deep well to top up Nottingham's reservoir.

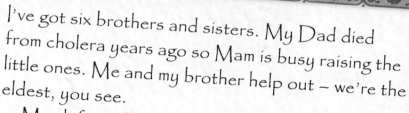

In a time when there were no free schools, poor children went to work. The wages helped their families survive. The working conditions were terrible. Here 12 year-old Constance Brown describes life at the Clifton coal mine in Nottinghamshire. Although imaginary this account is inspired by the lives of real Victorian children.

I have a bald spot where my head scrapes along the roof of the tunnel!

I've got six brothers and sisters. My Dad died from cholera years ago so Mam is busy raising the little ones. Me and my brother help out – we're the eldest, you see.

My shift at the pit starts at 5 o'clock in the morning and finishes at 5 at night. I'm a carrier. I pull loads of coal in a wagon from the coalface to the entrance, crawling on my hands and knees through a mile-long tunnel. I wear a belt and chain to pull the wagon. The belt cuts into my skin so I'm always sore. The coal is very heavy but I must be quick. If I fall behind with the loads, the miners beat me. I take morsels of bread or meat in my pocket to eat as I go along, because I'm not allowed to stop for a rest.

I hate the tunnels, so hot, dark and filthy. I'm black as tar by knocking-off time, with coal dust in my ears, up my nose and down my throat.

Sunday is my day off. I go to Sunday school, learning to read and write. Then I help Mam with the babies and cleaning the house. Like Mam says, "We're the lucky ones. We ain't orphans or beggars or now't."

This photo from 1987 shows the houses that were originally built for coal miners in Newstead Village. Notice how close they are to the pit.

Thanks to the invention of the camera, we have photographic evidence of life in Victorian times. This is Jesse Boot's store in about 1885.

Nottingham's last public hanging took place outside Shire Hall in 1861.

How do we know?

The Victorians were great researchers and record keepers. Nottingham Corporation kept records of its work in archives, telling us a lot about Victorian Nottinghamshire.

The Victorians also gathered evidence to help improve the lives of the poor. For instance, in 1842 there was an investigation into coalmining, including mines in Nottinghamshire. They interviewed child workers like Constance Brown. Their report resulted in a new law that stopped girls, women and boys under the age of 13 from working underground.

Mrs Anne Gilbert was four years old when she saw Nottingham Castle being destroyed. She wrote about it in her book 70 years later. Mrs Gilbert remembered the rioters as "a dense black mass of human beings, more like wild beasts, shrieking and howling." She described "columns of smoke" and flames "lighting up St James's Church, Standard Hill, and the whole neighbourhood." She wrote about the sounds of crackling fire and falling timber, the smell of burning wood and seeing the molten lead pouring from the roof.

Nottingham became one of the largest industrial towns in Victorian Britain.

CELT
500 BC

ROMAN
AD 43-410

ANGLO-
SAXON
AD 450-
1066

VIKING
AD 865-
1066

MEDIEV
TIMES
1066-14

Air Raid!

The terrible wail of sirens pierces the air, waking the children from their sleep. It's an air raid! Their mother runs in and cries for them to follow her. There's no time to change out of their pyjamas or grab their favourite toys. The family hurry to the Anderson Shelter at the end of the garden. They quickly climb down into the cold, damp interior. Nobody talks. Everyone is listening, terrified that they will hear the sound of bomber planes and explosions.

During the war, mashed potato was used for flour and whipped margarine was used for cream!

War Comes to Nottingham

Before World War Two, Nottingham was known as the 'Queen of the Midlands'. It was a large city with important industries and businesses. Although Nottingham had some of the worst slums in the Midlands, the future was looking bright. The war changed this. Men went off to join the army, children were evacuated to the countryside, and Nottingham's ancient caves found a new purpose as air-raid shelters.

The Germans targeted Britain's industrial cities to disrupt the war effort. On the evenings of May 8th and 9th 1941 the German air force launched the Nottingham Blitz. In total 424 bombs were dropped, killing 140 people and making 1,286 people homeless.

Luckily, a decoy fire at Cropwell Butler confused the enemy. Many of the bombs were dropped harmlessly in the Vale of Belvoir.

← University College on Shakespeare Street after the Blitz

TUDOR
1485-1603

STUART
1603-1714

GEORGIAN
1714-1837

VICTORIAN
1837-1901

MODERN
TIMES
1902-
NOW

Although not all children were evacuated from Nottingham during World War Two, many children were. Some families, however, sent their children to the countryside, where they thought it was safer.

Ten year-old Mary Jones has been sent to her aunt's farm near Cotgrave. The page on the right shows what she might have written if she had kept a diary.

At school we practise how to put on our gas masks, in case there's a gas bomb attack.

September 14th, 1941

I've been here three weeks now and I never thought I'd miss the streets of Sneinton so much! It must be tough on Mum. She works all day in the munitions factory and then goes back to an empty house. I wish I could help her but after the Blitz she sent me away – as far from Hitler's bombs as possible, she said.

The best thing about living with Auntie Jessie is the farm because I love being outdoors. I walk with my cousins for miles around the fields. Some cows chased us this afternoon – nasty brutes!

Auntie Jessie often gives us warm milk from the dairy. But thanks to rationing there aren't the usual ingredients at the grocers. For tea tonight we had omelettes made from dried egg powder. They tasted like cardboard! To make matters worse, there are hardly any sweets in the village sweetshop.

The village school is all right, but the other children don't talk to me because they think I'm an outsider. It's time for supper and bed now. Every night I pray for Dad, fighting far away. I really, really hope he comes home safely. The sooner this war is over, the better.

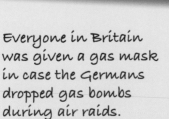

Everyone in Britain was given a gas mask in case the Germans dropped gas bombs during air raids.

CELT
500 BC

ROMAN
AD 43-410

ANGLO-
SAXON
AD 450-
1066

VIKING
AD 865-
1066

MEDIEV
TIME:
1066-14

Changing Times

After the war, Nottingham saw many changes. The lace and manufacturing factories began to lose business and industries had to change to be successful. The city council built lots of new houses, available for working people to rent.

In the 1950s and '60s many families from Commonwealth countries such as India, Pakistan and the Caribbean moved to Nottingham and Mansfield in search of work. Although there was some tension at first between the different cultures, most people soon settled in and made Nottingham their home. The city is now a mixed and lively community thanks to the different groups of people who have moved here over the years.

Notts County is the world's oldest football league club! It was formed in 1862.

SPOT THIS!

This statue honours Nottingham Forest's most famous football manager. He managed the club when they won the European Cup in 1979 and 1980. Do you know his name?

These girls are celebrating the Queen's Silver Jubilee in 1977. The old terraced houses around them were knocked down a few days later.

The University of Nottingham is one of the best universities in the country and is in the top 100 in the world.

New Jobs

In the 1980s Nottinghamshire's coalmines closed, like many others across Britain. Mining communities such as Mansfield and Kirby-in-Ashfield had to find new ways to make a living. Manufacturing companies also started to decline.

Today many Nottinghamshire people work for the government and other public services. The two universities have over 40,000 students and a large number of staff. Queen's Medical Centre opened in 1977 and is the largest teaching hospital in Europe.

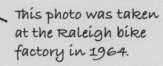

This photo was taken at the Raleigh bike factory in 1964.

Alan Sillitoe worked at the Raleigh factory and wrote a novel based on his experiences.

How do we know?

The 20th century has lots of historical evidence. Newspapers, film, radio and television provided more information than was ever possible before. For example, the damage done in the Nottingham Blitz was filmed and shown in cinemas. Photographs and film footage show us exactly what happened. At the same time, journalists interviewed witnesses for newspapers. After the war, television became the most important source of news.

All of these sources give us the facts. But sometimes fiction can help us understand history as well. A local author called Alan Sillitoe (1928-2010) wrote a famous book called 'Saturday Night and Sunday Morning'. It's about a worker in the Raleigh bicycle factory in the 1950s. The story describes the lives of ordinary Nottinghamshire people and the problems they faced.

Modern history has one other vital source. Many people who lived through the 20th century are alive now. Ask your parents and grandparents if they remember the Raleigh bike factory, the coalmines, or the football manager Brian Clough. You might discover something you never knew!

After the war, Nottinghamshire's industries started changing.

Nottinghamshire Today and Tomorrow...

Nottinghamshire's past is a story of change that can be discovered and enjoyed in lots of ways. The important thing to remember is that history is about the people who lived through difficult or exciting or dangerous times – people like Alec, Jane, Constance and Mary. How will our county continue to change in the future?

British athletes often come to Nottinghamshire to practise at Holme Pierrepoint's National Water Sports Centre.

The Raleigh bicycle factory is now part of the university campus.

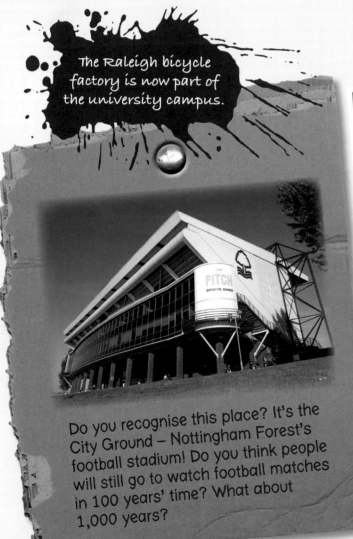

Do you recognise this place? It's the City Ground – Nottingham Forest's football stadium! Do you think people will still go to watch football matches in 100 years' time? What about 1,000 years?

Evidence of our industrial history is everywhere, from the Lace Market warehouses to Green's Windmill.

Nottingham's trams use electricity, not petrol, and are a fast way to get around the city. Do you think trams are a good idea?

Southwell Minster has been standing for hundreds of years. Do you think it will always be there?

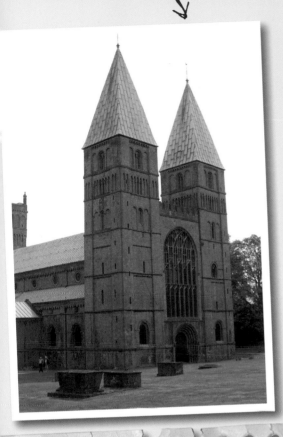

Nottingham is proud of its diversity. The New Art Exchange in Hyson Green displays the work of African, African-Caribbean and Asian artists.

The first bridge over the River Trent was built about 1,000 years ago. How long will today's bridge last?

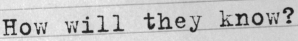

How will they know?

Will Nottinghamshire always look the way it does today? How will future generations know what the county was like for us, now? The Internet is a great way of recording the present. Photos, blogs and stories from tourists can all spread the word about our wonderful city. Who knows, hundreds of years from now someone may be looking at your picture or reading your blog. You're making history!

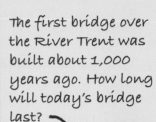

Feel proud to be a part of Nottinghamshire's future.

Glossary

Abbey – a Christian monastery or convent run by an abbot.

AD – a short way of writing the Latin words anno Domini, which mean 'in the year of our Lord', i.e. after the birth of Christ.

Anderson Shelter – an air-raid shelter used during World War Two, made from corrugated iron sheets and buried in the garden with earth piled on top.

Archaeologist – a person who studies the past by looking at the remains left by people in the past.

Battlements – a wall built around the top of a castle with regular gaps for firing arrows or guns.

BC – a short way of writing 'before the birth of Christ'.

Blitz – when the Germans bombed towns during World War Two.

Cavalier – the nickname for a supporter of King Charles I in the English Civil War.

Cholera – a deadly disease caused by filthy water.

Cremated – a dead body that has been burned into ashes.

Domesday Book – William the Conqueror sent his men all over England to check how much land and wealth was in his kingdom, and who owned it. The results of this survey were written in a book called the Domesday Book, which survives to this day.

Evacuate – to leave your home and go to a safer place.

Excavate – to dig out.

Friar – a member of a friary.

Friary – a place where men of certain religious orders of the Roman Catholic church lived.

Garrison – a place where soldiers stay.

Minstrel – a medieval musician who sang songs which told stories about distant places or about real or imaginary historical events.

Monastery – a place where monks live and worship.

Monk – a male member of a religious community that has rules of poverty, chastity and obedience.

Munitions – bullets and bombs.

Parliamentarian – another name for a Roundhead.

Plague – a serious disease that is carried by rats and can be transferred to humans by fleas.

Rationing – this controlled the amount of food and fuel people could use during World War Two in order to save resources.

Roundhead – anyone who fought on the side of Parliament against Charles I in the English Civil War.

Royalist – anyone who fought on the side of King Charles I in the English Civil War.

Index

Acknowledgements

The publishers would like to thank the following people and organizations
for their permission to reproduce material on the following pages:

p5: Galleries of Justice, The University of Nottingham Museum; p6: Fishbourne Museum, Chichester; p7: M. Todd. Nottingham University Dept Archaeology (No B1798), Fishbourne Museum, Chichester; p10: York Archaeological Trust, www.jorvik-viking-centre.co.uk; p11: York Archaeological Trust, www.jorvik-viking-centre.co.uk, Peterborough.Chronicle. firstpage-en, User, Geogre/Wikipedia; p13: Lenton Sands/Flickr; p15: The Art Archive/Alamy; p16: Andy Nicholson-www. nottshistory.org.uk; p18: National Fairground Archive, University of Sheffield, Andrew Phillips/flickr; p19: Oren neu dag (talk)-wikipedia; p20: Mary Evans Picture Library; p21: The Papplewick Pumping Station Trust; p22: Shane Phillips; p23: Boots UK Archive; p24: Manuscripts and Special Collections, The University of Nottingham; p25: York Museums Trust Castle Museum; p26: Roger Smith; p27: 10291066-Mary Evans Picture Library, B7N6CG-Geraint Lewis/Alamy; p28: Ian Douglas, John Sumpter @ JMS Photos; p29: Ian Douglas.

All other images copyright of Hometown World

Every effort has been made to trace and acknowledge the ownership of copyright.
If any rights have been omitted, the publishers offer to rectify this in any future editions.

Written by Ian Douglas
Educational consultant: Neil Thompson
Local history consultant: Philip Riden
Designed by Siân Williams

Illustrated by Kate Davies, Tim Hutchinson, Peter Kent,
John McGregor, Leighton Noyes, Nick Shewring and Tim Sutcliffe
Additional photographs by Alex Long

First published by HOMETOWN WORLD in 2011
Hometown World Ltd
7 Northumberland Buildings
Bath BA1 2JB

www.hometownworld.co.uk

Copyright © Hometown World Ltd 2011

ISBN 978-1-84993-173-1

CELT
500 BC

ROMAN
AD 43-410

ANGLO-SAXON
AD 450-1066

VIKING
AD 865-1066

MEDIEVAL TIME
1066-1485